RICHES
MY WAY

RICHES
MY WAY

Opening the Door to Financial Success

CRISTINA MARTINEZ

RICHES MY WAY
Published by The Cristina Martinez Company
1699 N. Capitol Avenue
San Jose, CA 95132
(408) 934-2000
richesmyway@cristinapowerhouse.com
www.cristinapowerhouse.com

ISBN 0-9778386-0-9

Cristina Martinez, Herna Mendoza, and John Burchfield are actual persons. However, the events and conversations they portray in this book are fictional. All other events and characters in this book are fictional, and any resemblance to actual events or persons is coincidental.

CONTENTS

[CHAPTER 1]

AN AMERICAN DAYDREAM

AS I PULLED OUT OF MY REAL ESTATE OFFICE onto Capitol Avenue, I glanced at the flagpole that stands rather elegantly near my company. As I noted the American flag fluttering softly in the breeze, I began to think about what America means to me personally.

I was born in the Philippines, and I had a good life there. But because of the particular circumstances that brought me to the States, I arrived here essentially penniless. I had the names of some people who had been recommended to me, and I hoped that my life would improve. I arrived in America just a day after Christmas. In a way, it was a thrilling time; but in another way, it was somewhat melancholy. Truthfully, I didn't have all the confidence in the world; but I did have hope.

After landing in Los Angeles on December 26, I went to the Social Security office the very next day so I could work in the United States and properly pay my taxes right away. At that time, there was nothing to prevent someone like me from immediately working in the United States as long as the paperwork was properly handled.

The next day, my host introduced me to the owner of a grocery store franchise in Los Angeles. He said, "This is Cristina Martinez. She's a chemical engineer from the Philippines, but you could hire her to do whatever you want her to do for you. The only thing that we are asking from you is to sponsor her so she can remain in America in good standing."

The store owner said, "She'll need to see an attorney, and I have one that she can use." We started going through the proper legal processes right away, and I started working that day in an Oriental grocery store.

To this day, I enjoy visiting an Oriental market. My daily work was difficult back then because I was the only employee who was assigned to clean fish. In Oriental food markets, it is, of course, customary for workers to clean, and even cook, fish for customers who request it. I spent many, many hours in the freezer processing all the fish. I washed them, displayed them, and took care of my customers.

In addition to handling the fish, I cooked for everyone I could. My employer asked, "Cristina, do you know how to cook?"

"Absolutely!" I answered. "Not only that," I said, "I can make more money for this store by cooking!" Stores lose a lot of profit if they have perishable foods like vegetables that spoil. In an effort to be industrious and to please my boss, I would keep tabs on our entire inventory. If I suspected any of the vegetables might be losing their perfect appearance, I might use them to create a delicious homemade soup. My customers would smell the aroma of the freshly prepared food, and they couldn't seem to buy enough of it. Instead of losing money by throwing away spoiling foods, we earned extra money by selling fresh, hot dishes.

Obviously, my employer liked the fact that I earned extra income for the store. But he also appreciated the fact that I was honest. In many of his stores, the cash registers were frequently short of cash because some of his cashiers were petty embezzlers. I always made it my goal to have my register balance to the penny. I beamed with pride when he said, "Cristina, in all my other stores, we have been losing money at the cash registers. But I've never lost a penny from your register, and I appreciate that!"

In the Philippines, I had always been energetic and industrious. Here in the great nation of America, I felt compelled to do even more. Not only was I frugal with perishable food and honest at the cash register, I did everything in my power to keep my store sparkling clean. It seemed to me that the cleaner the store was, the more customers we had; and I wanted to do everything in my power to make my store successful.

I remember thinking about the meat department. Just as the vegetables sometimes could easily spoil, after a couple of days in the display case, the beef and pork were not fresh enough to be sold uncooked; so I used every creative recipe I could find to make interesting dishes for the other store employees. In addition, I kept some of this cooked meat near my cash register and sold it to my customers. Once again, I was creating additional revenue for my employer.

Each time the owner came to our store, he complimented my entrepreneurial spirit. "What a great idea all this cooking is!" he said. Before long, we had a traditional Oriental market; but we also had all kinds of in-store cooking! Beef, pork, noodles, Louisiana blue crabs, and vegetable soup—we had a tremendous increase in food sales.

The owner was pleased with my work, and he continued to have his attorney work on my papers. At the time, I was making a meager $3.10 per hour. Though I was there from 8:00 in the morning until 10:30 at night, I was paid only from 9:00 to 9:00; and there was no overtime pay. After long, exhausting days on my feet, I would take the bus back home.

However, when I didn't want to spend my money for bus fares, I rose very early in the morning and walked a full hour to my store. There were times when it was very cold, and the coat I had was completely inadequate. But I felt it was my duty to sacrifice. I did what I could to be successful in that Oriental market, and I sent my family in the Philippines as much money as I possibly could.

It was tough, but I was glad for the chance to be in America. I retained my enthusiasm about being the best employee I could be. I prayed that all of my paperwork would be properly processed. Though I was sometimes tired, I always had hope. After all, I was in the dreamland of America, and I wanted to do my best.

To be honest, my job as a chemical engineer in the Philippines was far more prestigious than working in an Oriental market in the States. In some respects, my job made me feel ashamed. I didn't want my family back home to know what my day-to-day life was like here in America. I didn't want them to know that I was working in a grocery store cleaning fish.

So many of my friends back home thought of America as a nation of unbounded wealth. They thought, "If you're in the States, you automatically make lots and lots of money. In the United States," they thought, "money just grows on trees. You can have as much as you're willing to pick!"

Truly America is a land of unlimited opportunity. But, of course, it's not a place where you can become a millionaire just because you walk down the street. Even though I was doing my best as a clerk in an Oriental market, I knew there could be a brighter future for me. I wasn't completely sure when or how it would happen; but even when I was tempted to have my doubts, I kept my faith.

A little later, I had an opportunity to work in Northern California. When that happened, I experienced such magnificent opportunities that it is hard to describe all the blessings that began to fill my life. I was working in the real estate industry, and I had achieved financial freedom. My life now is something that only America and the goodness of God could have granted me.

The Stars and Stripes I saw gently undulating in the breeze that day had reminded me of my personal history and of the fabulous nation known as America. People the world over have heard of the American dream. As I was driving home that day, I experienced my own personal American daydream: the memories of my first days in this great nation, the memories of my humble beginning here, and the memories of how my simple life had been transformed into a life of magnificent blessings.

CHAPTER 2

A FEW DAYS TO RELAX

I HAD BEEN WORKING HARD to close 300 real estate deals in just a matter of months. In my business, I know a lot of real estate agents who live comfortably closing just one deal per month, and some of them even talk about how tiring work in the industry can be. I thought, "No wonder I'm tired! If I'm closing 30, or 40, or 50 deals in the same amount of time that a hard-working agent closes one, that's a good reason to be feeling weary!"

I found myself thinking about my friend Carol and her daughter Jan. I had known Carol for more than a decade, and I knew she and her family had been through some trying moments. I thought a few days of relaxation would help all of us. I called Herna Mendoza, my longtime business associate, and said, "It's time to relax! Call Carol to see if she and Jan can join us for a few days in Half Moon Bay! We'll get suites at the five-star hotel there, enjoy the beauty of the Pacific Ocean and spend *way* too much time at the spa. And we can shop till we drop!" As an afterthought I said, "Herna, be sure Carol knows she won't have to spend a dime. It's all on me."

"Carol has been a great friend," I thought. "I wonder which of my cars she would most enjoy driving?" Because I have been blessed with a booming business, I have a collection of beautiful automobiles. Not long ago, I purchased three automobiles in a single day. I bought a Bentley, an Aston Martin, and a Rolls-Royce Phantom. I can hardly pick a favorite, but it is fascinating to me that the Phantom is so exclusive that it is one of twenty-five in the world. It was an exhilarating experience to spend about three-quarters of a million dollars on three cars in a single Saturday afternoon—especially when I remember the days when I wondered if I would ever be able to afford a car at all.

"What do you think, Herna? Should we take the Phantom?"

"I don't think you can drive a sedan, Cristina," she said confidently. "With all the luggage we will have, we need to take the Hummer—or else drive two cars!"

"Yes! We will take the Hummer! And can you have someone take care of the hotel reservations? I want to have the very best rooms possible. I am looking forward to a couple of days of relaxation, and I want Carol and Jan to have a wonderful time!"

In what seemed like a matter of moments, we had booked two suites. The total cost of the rooms would be over $3,500 each day, but it would be worth it. I was looking forward to some time in a world-class resort, and I wanted my friend Carol and her daughter to have a terrific mini-vacation.

I could feel the stress and tension of my fast-paced business life begin to fade as soon as I started thinking about all the fun we would have as we made our great escape. All the information about housing availability, mortgage rates, and appraisals suddenly went to the back of my mind. Just thinking about the beauty of the ocean and the relaxed atmosphere of the resort was kind of a "mental massage." Sometimes, I love being spontaneous. I was looking forward to having a great time, and I was excited about relaxing with some of my friends in the charming little city of Half Moon Bay, California.

Suddenly, John Burchfield, the Executive Manager of my company, stepped into my office and interrupted me. "It's time for the carat count!" he cheerfully yelled.

"What do you mean by *carrot count?*" I asked.

John teasingly said, "Ladies and gentlemen, this is not the word *carrot,* as in a vegetable you eat. This is the word *carat,* as in the weight of a diamond! You don't become one of the most successful real estate agents in the world without having something to show for it. Cristina, we want to know how many carats of diamonds you are wearing on Wednesday, October 26. You know, just a typical day of the year. We want to have a carat count!"

"You're crazy, John!" I said.

"I may be crazy," he said, "but I still have my sense of humor, and I still enjoy having fun! Come on, Cristina. Let the count begin!"

Although I was standing in my own office, I felt like I was the guest on a corny television program. John had called in two of our staff ladies to assist him as he seemed to be assuming the role of a game show host.

"Don't miss a single one of them, ladies," John commanded. "Start with the ten-carat diamond ring, and don't miss those earrings! Get the bracelet, the necklace, the watch, the pendant—don't let her hide a single carat!"

"We're up to eighteen so far," one of the girls said with a laugh.

"Cristina, the necklace, the necklace. We need to know exactly how many carats of diamonds are on the necklace!" John demanded.

The whole situation was a little strange; but there was so much positive energy and goodwill in the room, I couldn't help but love it! I was grateful to have a staff that was so productive, but also fun loving.

"Hear ye! Hear ye!" John trumpeted in his deep, bass voice. "We have the final results of the daily carat count! May I have a drumroll, please!"

I couldn't help but appreciate John. Because of his management skills, our overall business productivity had quickly jumped by 85% just a few months after he began working for me. I wondered what kind of results he would be able to generate with the experience of another year. He was pleasant. He was readable. I never had to wonder what in the world might be going through his mind. But right now, it was not his management skill that I admired. I was admiring the fact that he hadn't allowed his success in business to rob him of the simple joys of life. He was a mature family man, but he still had the sparkle of a teenager!

John continued, "Today's carat count number is... 35!! Yes, you heard it correctly, staff. Cristina Martinez is wearing 35 carats of diamonds in this office today! That's right! The diamonds she is wearing today alone are worth more than many of the houses she sells. Come back again next time! Who knows, maybe tomorrow's outfit will push the carat count to 40!"

The next morning, Herna and I loaded our luggage into the Hummer at my home in Milpitas, California. I drove through the neighborhood, past the golf course, and soon exited the security gate. It is always soothing to see the valley from the hills. Though the Silicon Valley is one of the busiest, wealthiest, most productive places in the world, from high on the hills it all seems so gentle, peaceful, and relaxing.

I drove down the Montague Expressway until I reached De La Cruz Boulevard. Many of my friends live in the neighborhood near Greenwood Drive and Eastwood Circle, and I was soon knocking on Carol's door. When she answered, I said, "Are you ready to have some fun? All right!"

Carol is an energetic friend who is about my age. Because we were both born in the Philippines, we share a lot of customs and culture; and we even sometimes speak our native Tagalog language with each other. Carol is far from poor, but I knew her finances were a little strained at the moment. She and her handsome husband were heavyhearted because of some tough experiences. She was a person of character, a lady of dignity. And I wanted her to have a chance to break away from her own little world for a few days.

"Carol," I said energetically, "Put your luggage in my big Hummer, and let's go have some fun!" We loaded the car and began chatting like old friends do. No matter how much time elapses between each of my visits with Carol, we always pick up right where we left off.

As I drove down the San Tomas Expressway towards Saratoga, I noticed a little church on the corner. Most of the church is hidden from view, but the white steeple is clear to every car that passes by. Because I was with my friends on a trip that would be full of fun, friendship, luxury, and great times, I was reminded of God Who makes it all possible. My heart suddenly became very tender. In a single moment, I remembered so many stories of my childhood. I thought of all the blessings and all the pains. I was grateful that God has so generously provided for all my material needs. Not only that, but He also has given me enough to share generously with people who are important to me.

We had just passed Pruneridge Avenue, so I knew it was almost time to turn onto Saratoga Avenue. Since it was a vacation day, I found myself noticing things that would have otherwise escaped my attention. It was so pleasant to see the green trees lining both sides of the road. We passed many business squares and strip malls. On the sidewalk, a man and his wife were jogging while their dog ran playfully ahead of them. We seemed to drive by every possible kind of restaurant. At the edge of one of the parking lots, there was an old blue pick-up truck with a hastily soaped window that said, "For Sale! $1,650."

We drove through the scenic town of Saratoga and started zooming north on I-280. The vast difference between I-101 and I-280 has always amazed me. If I drive towards San Francisco on Highway 101, I feel the hustle and bustle of the Silicon Valley. But when I drive north on I-280, the vast expanse of the hills and the beauty of the gigantic clouds is staggering. The trees dotting the hillsides seemed to appear in just the right places.

As I exited onto Highway 92 towards Half Moon Bay, Carol noted the unique geographical beauty of the drive. "Cristina," she said, "did you know that people in ancient times believed that the whole universe operated in musical harmony? If that is so, it looks like the streams on the ground are performing a trio with the mountains and the clouds. The beauty is so real. Maybe nature is singing!"

"I agree, Carol," I said. "But it gets even better! When we get to our hotel, we will add the ocean, and then your trio will turn into a grand symphony!" I continued driving through the dazzling Santa Cruz Mountains.

"Half Moon Bay," the sign announced, "Population 12,500 and 70 feet above sea level." With the Pacific Ocean on one side and the Santa Cruz Mountains on the other, the little city of Half Moon Bay is, in many ways, a place where things don't change quickly. The city, founded in 1840, still shows signs of its Spanish heritage. The obviously aging bridge on Main Street proudly displays a sign that reads, "First Concrete Bridge Erected in San Mateo County, 1900."

All along the road, there are tree farms, flower shops, and stores that sell upscale landscaping products. Since we were arriving at the end of October, there were several pumpkin farms with signs *promising* that even the biggest pumpkin on the lot wouldn't cost more than five dollars.

The local residents, like most Americans, seemed to be passionate about local issues. Signs of every description seemed to show the value or the danger of certain political candidates. One large handwritten sign that said, "It's easy to criticize" seemed to be expressing why the local mayor should be re-elected. Nearby, another makeshift sign that said, "Take our town back" seemed to be explaining why the local mayor should *not* serve another term.

As we approached Highway 1, Herna observed, "We're almost there!" I turned south and followed the coastal highway to Mirror Point Road. Turning west once again, we soon arrived at the Pacific Resort, a newly built five-star resort with three golf courses, three magnificent restaurants, a spa, and luxurious rooms.

The well-tailored receptionist at the front desk said, "Welcome back, Miss Martinez."

Carol and Jan were a little surprised. "How did she know your name?" Jan asked. I was looking forward to introducing Jan to the world-class service that had made me a repeat customer of this outstanding resort.

When we got to our suites just past 1:00 in the afternoon, my room had a beautiful basket filled with fresh fruit and candy, a lovely flower arrangement, and a note from the manager that said, "Cristina, welcome back. We will do everything possible to make your visit pleasant and enjoyable."

As I read that note, I said to Carol. "You know, when I first came to America, I worked long, difficult days at a job that was physically demanding and exhausting. What a wonderful land of opportunity! I never would have dreamed that I could relax in such a wonderful place. I thank God for His goodness to me. Carol, I thank you, too. You've been such a great friend. I hope you enjoy every minute of your stay."

As all of us began to settle into our rooms, I called the spa to let them know we would arrive soon for our Pacific Resort Ultimate Treatment, their three-hour spa package designed to replace stress with feelings of calmness and well-being. I was already anticipating the drive to a nearby harbor later that afternoon to enjoy a sensational seafood meal. I had no idea, though, that I was going to meet someone who would add a whole new dimension to the restful mini-vacation I had impulsively taken. At the moment, all I knew was that I would be pampered for three hours at the spa. The hectic pace of my professional life was quickly fading into oblivion. I started daydreaming about the lavender wrap that awaited me downstairs.

CHAPTER 3

A CHANCE MEETING

AFTER AN EXTENDED SPA TREATMENT, I sometimes feel like lazily lounging in my room. But after the special treatment I had just enjoyed, I felt like going over to the harbor. I wanted to see the beauty of the sunset down by the boats and enjoy a meal in a restaurant that serves the freshest seafood imaginable.

Just after 6:00, we got into the Hummer and started driving back to Highway 1. We drove a few miles north until we reached Capistrano Road. Turning left, we were immediately in the beautiful area known as Pillar Point Harbor. People who love the ocean know that Pillar Point is a protected harbor. The harbor has an inner breakwater, but it also has an outer breakwater. Known as a rescue harbor, some claim it is one of the safest harbors in the United States.

But I was more interested in the sun that was just about to finish its journey and set for the day, casting beautiful hues of red, pink and purple over the gentle waves of the harbor. My eyes were captivated by the dozens of commercial fishing boats that charmed the bay. It was a postcard-perfect picture, and I wanted to soak it in.

We were walking towards the Harbor Side Restaurant. There might be a chef somewhere who could compete with Douglas Taylor's pan-fried perch, but I don't know where you would find one. With the fresh fish from that harbor and Chef Douglas's secret recipes, I knew we were about to enjoy a simply delightful meal.

Just as we were walking towards the restaurant, I noticed a bright white and red sign that said, "Fresh lingcod!!"

"Oh, let's go down to the boats," I said excitedly. "They still have some fresh fish for sale!"

When I was growing up in the Philippines, we had a custom of going to the market every day. So often, my father would say, "Who wants to go with me to the market?"

As a child, I was always a bundle of energy. If there was something to do, I wanted to be in the middle of it! Besides, I loved being with my father. So often, we would go to buy the fresh fish in the market, and I remember saying, "It's jumping! It's jumping!"

My father would say, "Oh, Cristina, this is going to taste great! I can tell this fish will make the best dinner of all!"

Although my father passed away many years ago, the joy and love he put in my heart is still there. And even though God has graciously lifted me from poverty and enabled me to become a citizen of a different nation, I still remember the simple pleasures of my childhood. While I was walking towards the white and red sign that was gently moving with the breeze as it advertised fresh fish, I was thinking how much I still appreciated the simple joy of being at a fish market.

As I walked down the ramp to the docking area, I saw a weathered seaman and his son. They were clearly hardworking people who loved the water. They had proudly christened their vessel the *Harbour Hawg,* and they had the best-looking lingcod I had seen for quite awhile.

"What are you doing?" asked Herna. "We're going out to eat, and you're here buying fresh fish! What are you going to do with it?"

"I'm going to take this fish to Chef Douglas, and he will cook it for me!" I said.

"You're crazy, Cristina. I don't think he wants to do that!" Herna said.

"If he doesn't want to, I'll pay him double—or triple! Then he'll want to!"

Talking to the fisherman, I said, "I want to make a meal for four. What's the best fish you have? Or do I need two smaller ones?"

He encouraged me to select two of the smaller fish, and his son busied himself packing them for me. "That'll be $40 even," he said.

"Here's $40," I said. As I added a few extra twenties and a hundred dollar bill between his two twenties, I thought, "This man and his fine son won't mind a little extra cash."

As our little group headed back up the ramp, just at that moment the fisherman called us and said, "Hey, lady. I think you paid too much!"

As I looked back to say, "It's for you and your son," a lady ran right into me just as I turned around to speak.

It was a real zoo for a minute! I had dropped my bag of jumping fish, and the lady who bumped into me had dropped her purse. Several items from her purse were rolling helter-skelter down the ramp, and we were all suddenly scrambling to keep her belongings and my fish out of the harbor!

When we had everything collected and the dust finally settled, I looked up to see one of the most charming ladies I had seen in a long time.

"Oh, I'm so sorry," she said kindly. "I suppose I was in a bit of a hurry, and I didn't really see where I was going. I hope you're okay!"

"Everything's fine," I said. "I just want to be sure my fish are all right! We are going to the Harbor Side Restaurant, and I am hoping to sweet talk the chef into cooking them for me."

"Well, I can take care of that," she said. "I was just taking a quick break. Actually, I'm one of the servers in the restaurant. Let me tell Douglas what happened. He's easygoing. I'm sure he'd be glad to take care of you. By the way, my name is Megan."

"I'm Cristina."

"I'm glad to meet you," she said. "I'm just sorry we met by accident."

A few minutes later, we were all seated at the Harbor Side Restaurant. Megan had convinced the chef to cook the lingcod we had just purchased from the *Harbour Hawg,* and she then appeared at our table.

"If you don't mind," she said, "I'd like to be your server this evening. I'd like to make up for my clumsiness on the ramp."

As the evening went on, I took the time to talk with Megan a little more. She really was a delightful person, and it was obvious that she was an excellent employee.

"How long have you lived here?" I asked.

"Actually, I've lived fairly close to here my whole life. I was raised just a few miles north of here in Pacifica. But when I got married about five years ago, Eric and I bought a little house in Half Moon Bay where he was raised. He had just finished at San Jose State with a computer degree, and he landed a good job that lets him do remote computer work from home. We both thought it would be great for him to be able to work here in Half Moon Bay."

"How did you start working at this restaurant?" I asked.

"It's curious that you should ask," Megan said. "When we were first married, I was working in the insurance field as an administrative assistant. I had already worked with that company a couple of years before we were married. I guess Eric and I both are pretty old-fashioned. We really pinch our pennies. We both did what we could to set aside money for a down payment for a house. When we got married, Eric was lucky enough to get a good enough job so that all my income basically went to paying back some loans to his parents and my parents. They had been good enough to help us put together a down payment."

"Yes, but how did you start working here?" I asked.

"Well, I was about to say that after a few years, all our loans got paid off; and I had the luxury of not working at all, at least for awhile. But, the man who owns this restaurant is a good friend of my husband's family. I don't know all the details, but there were some 'situations'; and they suddenly were shorthanded for help. My husband thought it might be a nice idea for us to help out old family friends, and I agreed to work a few hours a week."

"So you're just working here part-time?"

"Yes. To be honest, the wages are almost nothing; but I have been very fortunate to clean up on tips. But it doesn't really matter. I pretty much take all the money from this job and use it to help pay off our house a little sooner. Eric's a big one on paying down the mortgage. He said we could probably cut five, or maybe even ten, years off our 30-year mortgage. Then when we retire, we'll be in a lot better situation. You know, that's one of the things I love about him. He's a sweetheart, and he's really good to me; but he's so practical. The way he thinks about our future makes me feel secure about our lives together. So, Cristina, what exactly do you do?"

Before I had a chance to say a single word, Carol answered for me. "She's a millionaire maker!" she blurted out.

"Oh, my," Megan said. "What in the world?"

Carol continued, "Well, really, Cristina is a fabulously successful real estate agent. In fact, for four years in a row, she was the number one real estate agent in the world in a company that had thousands and thousands of agents all over the world. But though she buys and sells houses as easily as most of us buy groceries, she really is in the business of turning her clients into millionaires."

"Okay. I wasn't born just yesterday," Megan said. "You simply have to tell me the truth. It sounds to me like you're all making up a bigger fish tale than the locals tell here at Pillar Point Harbor. I've been set up too many times before. Tell me what's going on."

"Carol is telling the truth. I am a real estate agent in San Jose. To be honest with you, Megan, my business has been blessed so much—really, you and I have a lot of things in common. You're not working here because you have to. You're working here because you're trying to help out someone. Well, I have sold so many properties and I have so many investments, I don't go to work anymore to make money. I already have all the money I will ever need. What motivates me is that I want to help other people learn the easy secrets of investing in real estate. Carol called me a millionaire maker because I have the goal of making 1,000 millionaires before I retire."

"Wow, that's quite a goal," Megan said.

"Yes," I said, "but I have always had too much energy. When I was a little girl, my poor mother had such a difficult time keeping me quiet when we had guests. You know—I'm just bubbly. I want to do things! So I already have all the money I need, but I have too much energy to retire. What I'm trying to do now is to help other people reach financial freedom."

Megan said, "Well, my mom always said there are a few lucky people who strike it rich in business, and there are a few lucky people who win the lottery. The rest of us have to work hard!"

"It sounds to me like your mom had some good common sense," I said. "She's right when she says most people won't become millionaires by being lucky. But there are other ways of doing it, too. And you don't have to be a heart surgeon or a trial lawyer to become a millionaire. If you know the secrets and if you know the strategies, most hardworking people can become millionaires."

"Cristina, this really sounds too good to be true. And I've always been told that things that sound too good to be true usually are too good to be true. Is there some kind of catch?" Megan asked.

"Oh, I know exactly what you mean. This is not one of those things where you have to buy an expensive set of books—only to learn later that the plan won't work. This is not a gimmick. I can show you how to take what you have and turn yourselves into millionaires."

Then I caught myself! Here I was in a beautiful resort area trying to relax. And instead, I was talking business. But my business is so much fun, and it helps so many people. In a way, I don't always feel like I'm working when I'm sharing the secrets of financial freedom with people.

"I can talk to Megan," I told myself. "I'm not selling or buying a house, refinancing, making sure the inspections are done, etc. I'm just telling another very nice person how to be financially free."

"Megan," I said, "I can prove it to you—but not tonight. I'll make you a deal. Your husband works at home, right?"

"Right," she said.

"So he can make his own schedule, right?"

"That's right."

"And you don't ever work here in the morning, right?"

"That's right."

"Okay, let's all meet for coffee tomorrow morning, and I'll give you a hundred dollar bill for a tip. If you don't see the beauty of my plan after we've had coffee, I'll give you another hundred dollar bill for your time."

Megan was understandably taken by surprise, so she sputtered a bit, "Well. . .uh. . ."

"Okay, this is my last offer," I said. I pulled five hundred dollars out of my purse. Having financial freedom can be so much fun! "I have five hundred dollars for you and Eric if you'll meet me bright and early for coffee. Is it a deal?"

Megan joined in the fun, "Well, I'd be foolish not to accept all that money just for going to coffee. Sure! Do you want to meet at the Downtown Coffee Shop? That's the best one."

"That's where we will meet," I said. "Remember, I'm on vacation. When I'm on vacation, 'bright and early' means. . .11:30, okay?"

"Cristina, 11:30 is fine. But that is *not* bright and early. That's lunch time."

"No, no! I'm on vacation, so 11:30 is bright and early!"

We all laughed.

"So the millionaire maker strikes again!" Carol said. "Cristina," she said, "you do more work when you're on vacation than some people do on the job. No wonder you're number one."

"Let's eat in a hurry," I said. "I've got to get up bright and early for my 11:30 meeting!"

CHAPTER 4

DREAMS

I AM NOT SURE WHAT TIME the sun began shining on Friday morning because I was in no hurry to rush out of bed. When I finally did make it up, I found myself in the mood to order cheese blintzes with mango sauce and some delicious fresh pineapple. When the breakfast was delivered to my room, I asked to have my table set up on the balcony so I could take in the sights and sounds of the ocean while I leisurely enjoyed a meal.

It was a good thing that I had decided to meet Eric and Megan at 11:30. Any earlier would have been pushing it. As I was leaving the room to pick up my car, I met Herna, Carol, and Jan coming back towards the room from the hotel lobby.

"I'll be back in a few," I said. "I'm going for coffee with Megan and her husband."

"You sure have a strange way of relaxing," Carol said.

"Carol, you know I'm always in the mood to help people." I said.

As I headed down Main Street in Half Moon Bay, I passed Carter Park, so I knew the Downtown Coffee Shop was very near. I turned into the little strip mall, parked my car, and started walking towards the sidewalk. It was a pleasant setup. Attractive iron tables and chairs dotted the sidewalk outside the shop, and beautiful flowers and trees gave the place a pleasant sense of serenity.

Just then I spotted Megan and Eric coming out of the coffee shop. "Oh, I'm so glad you found us okay. My hardworking husband told me there was no Cristina, there was no five hundred dollars, there was no magic, and that I was just trying to get him away from his work!" Megan said with a teasing smile.

"So you're a real non-believer, Eric!" I said.

"Hi, Cristina, I'm Eric; and it would have been a little more pleasant to meet you if Megan hadn't spilled all my secrets before we even said hello."

We all laughed, and in just a few moments some of the special blends of coffee that were attractively displayed on the walls of the coffee shop had been turned into delicious drinks. And even a serving of the chocolate mousse cake from the pastry case made it to Eric's plate. We took a table outside where the sun was shining brightly overhead. We heard a few birds chirping and a few cars rolling slowly past the shop. Eric began with a question.

"Cristina," he said, "my mom and dad both worked regular jobs. They basically worked from eight to five every day, and we had a comfortable life. Dad always told me that God had given me a good brain, and that I should use it to get a job that was even better than the one he had always worked. I took his advice, went to college, and found a really good job. And Dad always told me to be careful about get-rich-quick schemes. He always said that the real joy of life comes from faithfully sticking to the basics: working hard, spending carefully, and being good to your family."

"Eric, it sounds to me like you have been blessed to come from a very good family. In a day when some parents do a pretty poor job of loving their children, you have been fortunate. But I believe a lot of the conventional wisdom about money is not truly wise. You should not be thinking the way ordinary people think because 90% of the people in our nation are working regular eight-hour jobs to get their paychecks so they can pay their bills. That's what the ordinary person is doing."

"Of course we pay our bills," Eric replied. "We're honest people. I always make my house payments and my car payments right on time."

"But," I responded, "the mere fact that you said you have a car payment means that you have bills. If you have bills, you are going to be excited about what I'm going to tell you. You see, when you have all those bills, you think of your eight-hour job. You already know how much income you will receive this month, and you already know the bills you'll have to pay. I will lay out a plan for you so you can enjoy more than your regular job can give you.

"The investments I show people earn money in three ways. When you work a job, you get paid one way; and it's taxable. But in my plan, you have a way to earn money besides just working a job."

"Cristina, you're scaring me," Eric admitted. "There are a lot of fast talkers out there, and it sounds like you're contradicting everything I've been taught about money."

"Eric," I said, "if you want to become financially independent, you have to be able and willing to become abnormal. Unfortunately, only a few people think that way. You know, there are so many places you can put your money."

"Sure, there are banks, stock mutual funds, retirement accounts, and so on," Eric answered.

"Let's choose three of the typical places where people put money. To keep the math simple, let's say you have $100,000. You can put it in a savings account. At today's rates, you might earn 1% to 3% in a savings account. So with an investment of $100,000 in a savings account that earns 3%, you would earn $3,000 per year. The money is safe, of course. It's insured. But the interest you earn is also taxable.

"Now let's think about stocks. Again, we'll start with $100,000. What is the rate of return on stocks? Well, some people say it's negative."

"It sure can be," Eric said. "I know some people who basically lost their retirement when the stock market took its last major downturn."

"Of course," I said, "but just for now, let's suppose that the stock market continues its overall positive direction and you earn 7% on your investment. So your $100,000 would earn $7,000, but you may feel that the money is not completely safe.

"Now, let's look at real estate. A recent newspaper article indicated that the annual rate of return on real estate in the Silicon Valley has been 18% to 20% over the past few years. In order to make you feel more comfortable, I won't even assume the best case scenario. If I use 10%, a more conservative number, it will still be hard to imagine the power of real estate investment.

"Let's suppose you bought a house one year ago for $500,000. If the house appreciated in value by 10% in one year, it would now be worth $550,000. But remember, you didn't spend $500,000 all at once when you bought the house. You might have spent a down payment of $100,000. So the amount of money you actually invested was $100,000, and the amount of money you earned through real estate appreciation was $50,000. Since you earned $50,000 on your investment of $100,000, your real rate of return is 50%. Is the investment safe? Of course it's safe. That's why it's called real properties.

"Eric, of course I'm talking to you about overall trends to illustrate my point. It's easy to speak of past trends, but I'm not a fortune teller! No one can make promises about future trends. But when you look at real estate statistics for the last 50 years, you will definitely see a consistent pattern of wealth building."

"So what you're saying," Eric questioned, "is that the conventional wisdom of investing $100,000 in a savings account would earn $3,000 in a year, and a lot of real estate investments could take the same investment and earn $50,000 in a year."

"Exactly! Now, is it taxable? Yes and no. Of course, you have to deal with good CPAs, but if you live in the house for at least two years, you have an exclusion of $250,000 for each person. So it's taxable at some rate over and above that. But remember that all the interest payments, the property taxes, and all the expenses are tax deductible. So if you had $100,000 right now, would you put it in a savings account, in stocks, or in real estate?"

"Well, based on what you said," Eric responded, "I would put my money into real estate."

"Of course you would," I agreed. "It's a no-brainer because no other investment can give you returns like this. So the real question is not whether or not you should invest in real estate. That's already settled. The question right now is 'how can I help you retire early?' "

"Being able to retire early would be a dream come true," Megan said. "I really admire Eric for all he does, but it would be great if he weren't tied down to a job. Then we could spend lots and lots of time together and travel all over!"

I knew that our conversation had led Megan to a very important place, the land of dreams. The big difference between rich people and poor people is the way they think. Basically, that's it. Being rich is not a matter of luck—many people who were "lucky" enough to win the lottery squandered all their money. They became poor again because they didn't learn to think correctly. Being rich is not even a matter of making a lot of money—many professional athletes earn enormous salaries, but not all of them have a lot of money once they quit playing. In a very real way, being rich is mostly about thinking right.

"Let me show you something, Megan," I said. "I'm going to write something for you to see. Once you see it, tell me what it says." At that moment, I took a very small sheet of paper and wrote on it:

IAMNOWHERE

"Look at this and tell me what it says."

Eric answered quickly, "That's easy. It says *I am nowhere.*"

"Yes, it does say that," I said. "But if you look carefully, you can read a different message."

"Oh, I see it," Megan said. "It says *I am now here!*"

"Precisely! You see, most of us are trained to focus on the negative. *I am nowhere* is a negative sentence. That's why a lot of us feel like we are *nowhere* in our finances."

"That's right," Eric said with growing agreement.

"But the sentence *I am now here* is a positive sentence, and I really want you to think about it. I want to congratulate you. Do you know that I love my work?

I actually enjoy talking with people and showing them a road map to riches. And though I don't do it every day, I have offered many people $500 for a chance to show them this road map. Unbelievably, many of them just won't do it. Right now, the two of you are already winners for being here; and so I want to congratulate you. You are at least interested in learning to think differently, in learning to think big, in learning to think like a rich person."

"Are you serious?" Megan said. "People actually turn down $500? They're that unmotivated?"

"In this world," I said, "most people are so trained to think small that they subconsciously push themselves away from thinking big. It seems that they have no ability to dream and to think big. But I know about the power of a dream."

As I was talking, I could see that both Eric and Megan were eager to learn; but they were struggling to imagine the possibility of living a different kind of life, given the resources they had. I decided to tell them a little bit of my personal story.

"Let me tell you about my first car," I said. "Back in 1983, I purchased a Toyota Corolla. I was so excited. I had saved money for three years in order to purchase that car, and I was so proud of it. I drove that car back and forth to work every day. Day by day, I would look at my boss who was 62 years old, but he could not retire. I began to think about my future. I realized that if I worked hard in that company and became a supervisor, if I did climb the ladder to reach his position—even if I did all that, I knew that I would not be able to retire in dignity. I worked at a good company. Though the salary they paid was enough to live on, it really wasn't designed to provide a comfortable, enjoyable retirement.

"That was a big turning point in my life. Then I learned some frightening statistics from the National Census Bureau. According to a United States Census report I once read, only 5% of Americans are financially free at age 65. The way I look at that, by age 65, 95% of Americans are either dead or dead broke! I knew one thing for sure: I didn't want to be in that 95% bracket. I wanted to be in the 5% bracket.

"So I started looking for more opportunities. I began working with an insurance man who retired as a billionaire. Not only did he show me how to earn a lot of money, he showed me how to think big. And that was very, very important to me. He showed me how to think outside the box. I know some people think it's crazy; but before you become wealthy, you have to see yourself as being financially free. You have to dream!"

"That makes sense to me," Eric stated. "In the world of work, you have to have the right mindset. If you don't think like an electrician, you won't be a good electrician. What you're saying is that if you don't think like a wealthy person, you won't be a wealthy person."

"Exactly! I believe that becoming wealthy is 80% mindset and 20% mechanics. Mindset is the way you think. The mechanics are the tools and strategies that you have to use to become wealthy. I believe that you become what you think about all day long. You'll never become wealthy without thinking like a rich person. You will stay poor if you think like poor people think.

"My first car was a rather modest vehicle. But just the other day I purchased an Aston Martin DB9. It's a V-12. It's the kind of sports car featured in movies and coveted by car lovers. Besides having plenty of nice cars, God, through His mercy and grace, has also blessed me with many other things. Besides the nice house that I live in right now, I am so privileged to be in the process of building a $15 million, 21,000-square-foot dream home that sits on five acres on a hill with a sweeping view of the Silicon Valley."

"Are you serious?" Megan asked. "You started out saving three years for a car, and this is where you are now?"

"Yes, I'm serious!" My excitement was growing. "Let me tell you more about the amenities of my new house. It will have a 360° view, an indoor pool, a spa, a steam room, a massage room, a gym, a game room, a theater that will seat 24 people, and a banquet hall that can seat 150 people. It has a beautiful circular driveway, and there's an underground garage for 12 cars. I only have 6 cars right now, so I'll continue adding to my collection. Outside, I will have a sports court and a tennis court.

"I also love vacationing in Hawaii, and I am so blessed to have seven investment properties there. I go there three or four times each year, and it's like a second home to me. I just bought two houses inside a resort that has a golf course overlooking the ocean.

"But you know what? In spite of all this, financial independence is not just about me. It's about helping people. It's about helping people like my family. I have been able to bring almost all of my family here to America from the Philippines, and I can't believe that. Besides, God has also given me the privilege of building a $3.6 million gymnasium and dining hall facility for a Bible college in Santa Clara. I believe in contributing to the community so young people can benefit, and I believe in giving back to the work of God.

"Not long ago, I sponsored a mission trip to the Philippines. In addition to having inspirational church services, we gave away 18,000 bags of groceries in one night. But you see, all these blessings started with just one thing—my first real house that I bought in 1984. I was able to use the equity in that house to achieve unbelievable financial goals.

"I wish I could impress upon your heart the fact that you have a lot of reasons to become financially independent. You can use your wealth for yourself. You can use it for your family. You can help people who need it, and you can choose which charities you want to support. In my life, all these things happened when someone taught me how to think big and how to dream big.

"I remember my mentor saying, 'Cristina, I don't want you to fly unless you fly first class. Think big. And I don't want you to go to motels. I want you to be in first-class hotels.' He told me to write down all of my dreams. And the blessings I have are some of the dreams I wrote down then. And some of the things I'm working on so passionately now are some of the dreams I wrote down back then.

"Right now, I'm giving about 30% of my earnings to my church; and I'm working on being able to give

50% of my earnings to my church. I want to do that because I believe everything that I own belongs to God because He's the one who gives me the health, talent, and ability to do my job. I'm not getting poorer by giving away so much. I'm getting richer and richer and richer. I am so happy giving!"

Megan seemed stunned. "Are you saying that you were basically in a financial position like we're in right now, but your dreams carried you to this fabulous wealth you've just described?"

"Yes, that's exactly right. And soon, I want to purchase a private airplane. And through my business, I want to create 1,000 millionaires. I have already made 100 of them. Now here's the first step. Take a moment to do this exercise. I call it the Dream Sheet."

I handed a piece of paper to both Megan and Eric. "Here's what I want you to do. I'll give you two minutes to write down as many dreams as you can. Be wild. Write down your wildest dream. The only rule is that you have to keep writing. You can't stop to think and reflect. You have to keep writing.

"I want you to write down the places you want to go to, the vacations you want to have, the houses you want to live in. Write down the kind of car you want to drive. List the people you would help and the charities you would support. Write down the children you would want to put into college. Who would you help if you became a millionaire or a multi-millionaire? Dream big! It's very important to dream big.

"Remember, we're changing our mindset. Write down some things that seem impossible to obtain. That's what dreaming is about, and it works. No one ever learned the mechanics to make dreams come true without first having a dream."

Eric and Megan smiled at each other, and then they began writing. "I want to see who the winner will be," I said. "Who can write the most dreams?"

Soon, they had each filled a page with their dreams. They had identified what seemed really important to them.

"It's so strange," Eric said, "I almost feel that I don't have permission to accomplish some of these things. But just thinking about my dreams and writing them down seems to give me a sense of energy, and a sense of liberty."

"That's really terrific," I said. "I can show you a road map to riches, but I doubt you'll ever follow the path unless you first have some dreams. But let's make a deal. I have really enjoyed your company, but I want to go back to my hotel now and spend some time with my friends. I'll give you the $500 now, but let me give you some investment strategies tonight. Why don't the two of you spend some time this afternoon dreaming about what your financial future could be and then join us for dinner tonight? I'm sure you'll love the food. The restaurant at our hotel didn't earn a five-star rating for nothing! Let me go relax for a while, and then we'll talk more during the meal. Is that a deal?"

"So far," Megan said, "you have done nothing but make us offers that we cannot refuse. Wow! The next time I go to work, I'm going to be looking for multi-millionaire real estate agents to bump into!"

We all laughed and began to leave the table.

"Dinner will be at 6:30, Megan. And I want you and Eric to come hungry!"

With a smile and a wave, we were off. I was going back to a beautiful resort, but I was confident they were going somewhere they had never been: the land of dreams.

CHAPTER 5

STRATEGIES

ON FRIDAY AFTERNOON, Herna, Carol, and I went shopping. I was eager for Jan to come along with us, but she couldn't resist the spa. While she enjoyed several hours of being pampered, the three of us started through the nearby shops.

"There are rules for shopping today," I announced energetically.

"Rules! How can any woman follow rules when she's shopping?" Carol teased.

"Today, I have the thousand-dollar rule, and I'm serious about it." I knew Carol had no idea what I had planned to do, but I wanted to experience the joy of giving. Carol was a dear friend, and I wanted to encourage her and lighten her heart.

"Here's the thousand-dollar rule. I will give you one thousand dollars cash, and you have to spend it all! As soon as you run out of money, you have to get a fresh supply of cash. Every time you get a fresh supply of cash, it's another thousand. And if you don't get lots of 'refills,' it means you're not a good friend. And you're a good friend, right?"

"Cristina, you are out of control," quipped Carol. "You can be so outrageous! But at the same time, you're so much fun. Okay, okay! I submit to the rules of shopping for today!"

We started making our way through dress boutiques and jewelry shops, antique stores and furniture shops. After a few hours, we had packages everywhere. With my never-ending passion for jewelry, I was thrilled to find a bracelet that was exactly what I was looking for. It had eighteen carats of brilliant round diamonds set in yellow gold, and it sparkled beautifully in the sunlight.

Herna began to prod us. "We've got to get moving," she said, "or we won't be on time for dinner. Besides, someone has to rescue Jan from the spa!"

We all laughed and began an unhurried walk back to the car. I began thinking about the meal and said,

"Tonight, I'm going to have the freshest fish possible! I can't wait to see what the chef is cooking up today!"

Although we had plenty of time, it seemed that just a few moments had gone by when we met up with Megan and Eric. As we entered the hotel dining room, I was impressed with the breathtaking view of the Pacific Ocean and the way the colors of the setting sun gave the restaurant a wonderful sense of warmth and charm.

I was eager to try the appetizer of baby calamari stuffed with chard, but I knew Eric would probably appreciate something a little more ordinary. "Eric, if you started off with the salad they're calling baby organic greens and added those roasted corn crab cakes, I think you'd enjoy your filet mignon a lot more!"

"That sounds good to me," Eric said, "but I was thinking about being a little more adventurous and trying the pumpkin soup just because it sounds different."

"Well, my Filipino roots are taking over; and I'm having seafood all the way!" I announced. "I'm going to start with the calamari, and then I'm going to have the slow-roasted salmon that comes with bok choy and matsutake mushrooms. But it doesn't matter. Everyone will have what he wants, but save plenty of room for dessert!"

Soon the business of ordering the meal was taken care of, and more earnest conversation began. Eric was in a questioning mood.

"Cristina, Megan and I spent some time this afternoon dreaming about possibilities for the future. Dreams are good things. But how do you find a way to turn those dreams into reality? Are there strategies?" he asked.

"Eric, people have become wealthy a lot of different ways. But for the typical worker who has good enough credit to own his own home, I have a road map that has worked really well for a lot of people.

"In all likelihood you and Megan have a lot of money in your house, and I can show you how to get the equity in your house working for you. But most people don't think this way. Eric, what are the things most people think of when they think of their house?"

"Taxes!" he exclaimed. "Taxes, house payments, and repairs."

"Yes," I agreed, "all of that is part of owning a home. But the repairs of a home are very minor compared to the equity of the home. With me, I don't think of a house as a matter of taxes and mortgage payments. I think of a house as a gold mine, a sleeping giant. Eric, you and Megan have a sleeping giant in your house. And you need to wake up that sleeping giant and get him working for you."

"In a way," Megan said, "it still seems a little vague. In the real world of money, how do you go about waking up what you're calling a sleeping giant?"

OPTION ONE

"Okay. You and Eric are very conservative, and you own one home. You're trying to pay it off. So let me give you some options, and I will be done. I will be very, very clear here. Let's say you own a home and you've been trying to pay it off early. Perhaps you tried to accelerate your mortgage by taking out a 15-year mortgage at an interest rate of 5.5%. Now you have a loan balance of $200,000. At this point, perhaps your mortgage payment, including the principal and interest, is $1,600 per month.

"Now, suppose that the market value of the property is now $650,000. That would mean you have $450,000 in equity. So I see that as a sleeping giant. If this is your situation, I could do what I call Option One. What is Option One? Option One is very, very conservative. That is when you refinance the house, take some cash out, and buy something."

"What would I buy?" Eric asked.

"You buy a second property. If you have good credit and a good income, the bank will give you a loan of up to 80%. That means they will loan up to $520,000 for a house valued at $650,000. If you only owed $200,000, that means you could take out as much as $320,000. I recommend that you take out some equity and put it to work immediately.

"Where would I put it? First, because I'm giving you the most conservative option, I would simply put it into a single investment property that will generate monthly cash flow. Your investment could pay for itself as a rental with a minimum down payment of 20%. But since you have enough equity available to put down 30%, I have good news! Your profit on this rental property will be about $1,000 per month. This is positive cash flow for you and Megan!

"The investment property I'm thinking about for you right now would only require a down payment of about $265,000 to get you this positive cash flow. And you already have more than this available in your home equity!

"Think about it. If you invest that amount, you're starting on your road to riches. The way I see it, what are you waiting for?"

Eric and Megan seemed to be following the concept well, and the numbers were making sense to them. "In our area," Eric said, "rents have been lower the last few years. What does that mean?"

"In the years before Alan Greenspan retired from the Fed, there was a time in America when interest rates were very, very low. This circumstance made it possible for huge numbers of renters to become home owners. As tenants were converted to home owners in record numbers, the rental pool shrank in our area; and the law of supply and demand made the income of rental units go down a little.

"Though it may be hard to understand, one of the best times to purchase rental units is when the property rents are down. I can explain more of those details later.

"In the example I just mentioned, the one that generates $1,000 per month—well, those numbers were much higher before the tragic events of 9/11. Before that time, some of our investors were earning $2,500 per month on similar investment properties."

About that time, the appetizers arrived at our table; and the aroma of the freshly prepared food was wonderful. The calamari was so perfectly tender. This was truly a magnificent place for a meal.

"Once you have begun investing with Option One, I would recommend that we diversify your portfolio into other investments when you have earned sufficient equity.

"Now keep in mind that long-term investments earn money three ways. The first source of income is from the cash flow itself. This money comes to you each month, and it's one way your money is working for you. The second source of income is from the property appreciation. In the Bay Area, many income-producing properties went up in value by at least $100,000 last year. In other words, not only do investors earn the monthly income, they also earn money from the increasing value of the property. The third source of income is from the tax benefits. Investment properties are a tax shelter. One of the factors is depreciation, and this is something you can do for decades. Besides, all the expenses you incur are tax deductible."

At this point, Eric seemed slightly put off. "That sounds good, but it's not exactly easy to become a property manager."

"Eric," I explained, "a lot of people don't want to manage properties. That's why I started a property management company to help investors with all that. And believe me, there are plenty of property management firms if an investor is uncomfortable with mine. In many cases, these properties may double in value within a few short years, depending on their location. And when that happens, you can refinance and purchase even more properties. You see, the goal is to acquire as many properties as possible because this is the path to retirement."

Megan seemed slightly troubled and said, "But why were we always taught that getting ahead meant just trying to pay off our house early?"

"Paying off your house early is good, but it's not the best plan. If you pay off your house, your money is in your house sleeping. Meanwhile, you have to keep working in order to make the payments. But if you are committed to paying off your house, wait until you own several properties. Then you can pull out some cash and pay off the house. I don't generally advise this because it's an easy way to get hit with a huge tax bill.

"As your investments keep growing, you will be able to acquire commercial properties. That's where the real cash flow is! And that will give you the retirement money you need. Many commercial properties are set up so that the tenants pay all the expenses of the property. The tenants pay the taxes, the insurance, the utilities, the maintenance, and the management. Basically, the only obligation for the owner is the principal and the interest."

"Wow!" Eric said. "I'm beginning to see a long-term picture here. If I follow a good plan, the equity in my house can begin working for me. After a few years, I can own properties that will give me a substantial monthly income."

"I'm glad you're seeing it. Let me tell you something about my own life. I own a few commercial properties; and on just one of them, I earn $43,000 every month from my investment. Believe me, that's a lot of money, and it's hard to spend! So it's clear that commercial property is the name of the game, but you have to reach this phase step-by-step. You have to do it phase by phase."

Eric seemed to be thinking through the numbers carefully. "Please help me understand," he asked. "As far as getting out of debt is concerned, if someone followed the plan you outlined, he would have started with a mortgage of $200,000; but he would have ended up with a mortgage for $465,000 on his original property, plus a mortgage on a second property. Is that really going to help over the long haul?"

"Eric, you need to begin to think about finances in a creative way. Remember, so much of being wealthy is all about mindset. Let's suppose the refinancing was done with a 1% adjustable-rate mortgage or with a 5.5% fixed-rate mortgage. The adjustable-rate mortgage would have a payment of about $1,673 each month, and the fixed-rate mortgage would have a payment of about $2,167 per month.

"Now because you put the $320,000 equity in two properties and one of those produces an income of $1,000 each month, that $1,000 of income each month means the amount of money you have to come up with each month for your mortgage is only $673. I don't know about you, but I'd much rather have two properties that I had to pay $673 each month for than have one property with a mortgage payment of about $1,600 per month. To me, that's a no-brainer. And that is Option One, a very, very conservative approach."

As we continued talking, our main courses came. It was really great to see six handsomely dressed waiters at our table so the silver coverings for our plates could all be lifted at exactly the same time. The beef presentation looked particularly pleasing because the filet was garnished with braised short ribs, a medley of fall vegetables, and a truffle-potato puree. As we began enjoying our meals, I continued talking with Megan and Eric.

MORE OPTIONS

"As good as Option One is, there are options I like even better because they have the power to get you into the fabulously profitable world of commercial property much faster.

"Not long ago, I had some clients who had lived in the same house in San Jose for 23 years. After all those years, their house payments were so small it seemed incredible. I encouraged them to try this option, but they were nervous and they resisted. I remember saying, 'Let me tell you something. You're nervous, but I'm not nervous. If I get nervous, that's when you should get nervous.'

"So, about a year ago, they agreed to take the steps I outlined. By following just one of my more aggressive investment strategies for them, they increased their net worth by $600,000 in just one year. That kind of dramatic growth in wealth would not have been possible with the more conservative approach I described to you as Option One. Now, they're ready for me to take them through the next steps. Their decisions are helping them enjoy a wonderful retirement."

"That seems unbelievable," Megan observed. "You're saying these people followed your advice, and they're making money hand over fist! You must tell me the details!"

As I began to explain the absolutely incredible investment strategies that are available in the world of real estate, I rather lost track of myself. Suddenly I produced blank papers from my purse and began to use them as my chalkboard. Ideas were flying. Numbers were bounced around. And by explaining the details of Option Two and the even more aggressive possibilities of Option Three, I could see Eric's eyes brighten with enthusiasm.

As I continued talking, I was afraid that my little speech was going to draw a crowd! I have seen so many people's financial destinies completely transformed that I am a true believer in these plans. Even our waiter, though he maintained his professional demeanor, was doing his best to listen. When the truth of real estate investment is expressed plainly, it generates passion, hope, and excitement.

As I told Eric and Megan the details of the plan, they were absolutely enthusiastic. At one point, Eric said, "The thing I like so much about all the options you're presenting is that they make complete sense. This is not some kind of smokescreen or some kind of magic. It's just creative, logical thinking that will obviously work!"

"You see, it's not always about what you have," I said. "It's about how you use what you have. But before the evening gets away from us, I'll tell you even more."

Eric took a little break from the real estate conversation and said, "Cristina, thank you so much for this meal. I have to say that the chef put together a remarkable combination of flavors."

"Yes," I said, "but I warned you to save room for dessert. I'm really having a hard time deciding between the molten chocolate cake and the chocolate trio which includes a delicious Swiss chocolate ice cream."

Megan smiled teasingly and said, "If you can't choose, don't. Just get them both!"

"My wallet can afford it, but my waistline can't!"

SENTIMENTAL VALUE

Just then, Eric brought up an interesting idea. He said, "I think my parents would be hesitant about some of the plans you're describing, Cristina. To them, their home has a lot of sentimental value. But more than that, the financial ideas they have had through the years give them a certain level of comfort. I think they're sometimes tied to sentiment in a way that is not financially beneficial to them."

"Eric, I have an interesting approach—not one I highly recommend—that I use for people who have strong sentimental feelings about their homes. Of course, when it comes to early retirement, sentimental value has no value at all! But there are people who do think and feel this way." Teasingly, I said, "It almost makes me cry, but only when I think of all the money they're losing!

"Anyway, I have thought through plans that help people who are controlled to some degree by their strong sentiment. Though my approach with these people doesn't necessarily build their equity as fast as some other approaches do, I have thought of a way of waking up the sleeping giant of their home equity. There are ways of accommodating their strong emotional feelings and sentiments, and still getting them to a place where their money is working for them."

Megan said, "I can see why some people would become emotionally attached to their homes. At the same time, I can see how those feelings could limit their financial choices. I guess it would be better to get them doing something they feel comfortable with than to have them do nothing at all."

"Megan and Eric, I believe the options we have discussed are the best and fastest way for people to become financially free. It's the best way for people to become wealthy and to retire early. And quite frankly, I know it works because I have done it. I'm still doing it. And I have done this for hundreds of my clients. There are many things I don't know. As a matter of fact, I'm sure you and Eric both know many things I don't understand at all. But I do know how to get rich in real estate. I know a lot about real estate investments, and I have helped a lot of people become millionaires through real estate investments. I've already been through three recessions, and I've never lost money in real estate. Housing prices dropped back in 1983. When the next recession came in 1990, the housing prices dropped again—but not as low as they had been in 1983.

"Most people would like to have $43,000 coming in every month, but they have to take the right steps to get there. Most people would like to own enough income-producing property that they didn't have to worry about their home mortgage any longer, but they need to use some of the options I have described to reach that level of financial freedom.

"By placing a few phone calls, I could let you speak to dozens of my clients who followed this road map to riches and became multi-millionaires. Frankly, they would still be depending on their eight-hour-a-day jobs to keep the bills paid if they hadn't followed these strategies."

These thoughts seem to take hold in Eric's mind, and he responded, "When I was in college, there were some students who seemed to sail through, even though they didn't necessarily have unusually high I.Q.'s There were others who always struggled getting things done, and many of them eventually dropped out. When I played basketball in high school, some of the athletes just seemed so natural; but there were others who had such negative attitudes that they seemed to defeat themselves. They seemed to have the ability, but it was blocked. In both school and sports, there is a 'qualifying mindset.'

"What you're telling me, Cristina, is that there is also a qualifying mindset for financial freedom. And it seems to me that someone could have a brilliant mind for schoolwork, but not know this; and his good grades wouldn't necessarily make him rich. And someone could have an aggressive attitude that works great for sports, but not know this; and his athletic mindset wouldn't necessarily make him rich. But when you have the right mindset for finances—and when you have the right strategies—you can actually take the steps that lead to financial freedom."

"Megan and Eric!" I exclaimed, "This is the best deal of your life. I've shown you the road map to riches, and I'm paying you $500 for teaching you principles that can lead you to wealth and early retirement."

"You know, Cristina, I truly was a non-believer when Megan told me about this far-fetched deal. But now that I see how you are approaching all this, I can understand that it's truly possible for us to start down a path that will help us accomplish the financial goals we have. Please accept my thanks for all your generosity. The money. The food. But more than that, thanks for sharing your knowledge. I'm so glad you and Megan literally bumped into each other at the harbor. I think it's going to be something that changes our lives."

After a nice day of shopping and visiting with new friends, I wanted a long, relaxing massage; but I wanted to be in my room. As we were leaving the restaurant, I stopped by the concierge desk and asked, "Do you have a massage therapist that can come to my room?" It didn't really matter how much it cost. Real estate investing has provided me with financial freedom, and I am able to enjoy the rewards and blessings of good decisions I made years ago.

CHAPTER 6

FINANCIAL INTELLIGENCE

I AM NOT REALLY A MORNING PERSON. When I need to be, of course, I am on time for morning business meetings. But I don't love mornings; and when I can, I enjoy starting my day a little later.

But if there is one thing that can motivate me to get moving in the morning, it is a farmer's market. I enjoy shopping, but I especially enjoy shopping for fresh food. If I'm at a market early on a Saturday morning, I will go to the pier and buy everything the fishermen have. Fresh squid, shrimp, crab, lobster, fish—I take the whole nine yards!

There is a farmer's market near my home, and we often dash in there after church on Sunday. I tell the vendors, "I'm sorry that we're coming at the last minute. I know we're not even dressed right for this place because we're rushing here from church. But if you'll give me a quick bargain, I'll move on so you can close."

Then we begin to bargain. They sometimes let a whole box of eggplants go for $4. I like to see the fish—especially if it's early enough in the day that they haven't started to stink yet! If there is a line, I will look for someone who seems approachable and say, "Okay, I'll buy you everything you want, plus extra. All you have to do is buy fish for me because I'm in a hurry!"

Part of the reason I like the farmer's market so well is because I enjoy cooking. And nothing is better than cooking with the freshest ingredients possible. I spent many hours catering meals as a young adult, and I still enjoy the art of cooking.

I have enjoyed purchasing investment properties in Hawaii partly because of the fabulous farmer's market there. It reminds me of my childhood in the Philippines. There, we didn't have refrigerators, so we bought fresh food each day. My dad would say, "Okay! Who wants to go to the market and buy the food for today?"

I always said, "I will! I will!" The market near our home in the Philippines was always very wet, so we had to wear storm slippers while we shopped. I remember seeing all the fresh fruits and vegetables. And there were always some jumping shrimp that delighted my young eyes. When we bought pork and beef, the animals were all hanging right there because they were freshly killed that day. My dad would say, "Give me that part, and be sure to slice it thin."

Even now, when I visit a good market, it makes me feel like a child in the Philippines all over again. I have even driven all the way to the market in San Francisco to purchase live chickens and driven all the way back home with them so I could have fresh chicken for dinner!

And so, on this lazy Saturday morning in Half Moon Bay, I decided to drive to the farmers' market on Main Street. I had told Eric and Megan that I was going, and I was kind of hoping they would be there.

I drove to the parking lot just behind the Mediterranean restaurant where the market is held each Saturday morning. At the edge of the parking lot near the restaurant, a young man was gently strumming a guitar and singing. At the same time, a cheerful vendor was holding up some fresh greens and saying, "I'll give you a pound for a dollar! This is the best time of year for these! Fresh? They were just picked yesterday!"

Another vendor was offering fresh carrots for $2 a bunch and telling everyone that pigweed was absolutely wonderful in tossed salads, and that the chard was really great in minestrone soup. Underneath a bright blue tent, a vendor stood near his yellow cooler listening to a young mother say, "My father's coming in tomorrow, and he's an artichoke fan."

"Well, buy him some!" the salesman insisted.

Just at that moment, the lady's young son, entirely missing the fun of the market, said, "Mom, can we go to the grocery store now?"

As the lady started dealing with her son, she forgot to pick up the artichokes she had just purchased. The salesman said, "You leave those here, lady, and I'll re-sell 'em!"

Just then, I noticed Eric and Megan walking towards the market. "How are my investors doing today?" I yelled out to them.

"We're doing great," Eric said loudly. "We heard that a millionaire maker was going to be here today, and we wondered if we would find her by the carrots or by the tomatoes!"

"Well, one thing is for sure. I'll be going home with lots of fresh food. And I may drive back to the harbor and take home some fresh fish, too!"

Megan seemed to be in particularly good spirits and joked, "To be honest, Cristina, we never really thought about the fact that some of the customers at this simple farmers' market might be totally loaded multi-millionaires! In so many ways, you're just like us; but in so many ways, you're totally different."

"It's all about financial intelligence," I noted.

"Financial intelligence—what does that mean?" Eric questioned.

"In the first place, financial intelligence has to do with a positive mindset. We've already talked about that. It has to do with a person's ability to dream for a better reality than he currently has. In a lot of ways, many people are living self-fulfilling prophecies. At the very best, they imagine themselves as living middle-class lives; and they cannot picture themselves being financially independent. Because they have no dreams for financial freedom, they don't take any of the necessary steps for financial freedom. That's why I think they are living a self-fulfilling prophecy."

"But a positive attitude alone can't produce great wealth," Eric said.

"Of course not. There has to be a strategy. But 80% of financial intelligence is the proper mindset, and only 20% has to do with strategies like we talked about last night. I once heard a preacher say that what you do with Christ in a moment can affect your whole eternity. I believe that. And I also know that people can make a few decisions in a matter of moments that truly change their financial destiny."

"Can you give me some concrete examples of that?" Megan asked.

"Absolutely. Just recently a middle-aged man came to my office. He was highly educated; and, in his own way, you might think he was a relatively successful person at his job. One year ago, he purchased a condominium that he used as a rental property. Now, he is ready to sell that so he can purchase a single-family residence.

"As we talked through some of the details, he told me he had worked hard at his job all year long. He estimated that he had worked 3,000 hours at a bare minimum. Yet, he had only 'worked' on his rental property for about 5 hours that year, including the time it took him to sign all the papers. But with only 5 hours of work, he had earned more money than he had in 3,000 hours of working for his employer. Making a profit of $70,000 with an investment of only 5 hours—that's $14,000 an hour! That's an example of financial intelligence."

"It's really incredible when you look at it that way!" Eric exclaimed.

"Now, because of this man's financial position, he was able to do that only one time during the year. He simply didn't have enough money to purchase two properties instead of one. But the difference between him and the average person is that he did have the financial intelligence to invest those five hours. He made a decision in a matter of moments that has changed him into an investor. If he keeps that up, the decisions he makes in a matter of moments will earn him more money than the job he works full-time.

"The nice part about it, of course, is that his financial intelligence enables him to work a job he really enjoys. But at the same time, his personal financial possibilities will not be limited by his position. Besides that, when it becomes time for him to retire, he will have many, many more options."

"I suppose you know a lot of stories like that," Megan said.

"My list goes on and on. A few years ago, an engineer came to my office. I suppose he and his wife were about 60 years old at the time. His professional career had been spent in the aerospace industry. He owned a house in the Bay Area, but he could not retire. His wife had read an article about me in a local newspaper that claimed I had the 'Midas touch.' They came to meet me because the article claimed I could turn ordinary homeowners into owners of multiple properties.

"When they came to my office, they looked very, very conservative. They had never spent a lot of money on an expensive car. They were not glitzy, flashy people. Their financial ideas were conservative as well. They didn't want to touch their 401K. They didn't want to touch the equity in their home. They wanted to pay off the mortgage so they could have enough money to retire.

"When they came to my office, they thought that they might consider buying one additional house. After one hour, they decided to purchase two houses.

Now, a few years later, their retirement is funded by the multiple apartment complexes and income-producing commercial property they own.

"So they were the kind of people who read the newspaper, and they talked to each other about their financial situation. It may have taken them 30 minutes to drive to my office. We may have talked for an hour, maybe an hour and a half at most. But they listened with an open mind. They used their academic intelligence to evaluate what I was saying and to realize the great potential in my strategies. Finally, they took heed to what they had been told. In a way, they stepped out by faith. And in a few hours, the character of their retirement changed from being rather dismal to being incredible and awesome. That's financial intelligence."

Megan was curious. "Do you know any stories about people who didn't have a lot of general intelligence, but they seemed to have a lot of financial intelligence?"

"It's strange that you should ask me that question," I said. "Just recently, I met with a lady who was in terribly difficult circumstances. I suppose she is about 53 or 54 years old, and she had just lost her job. Her husband is a few years older than she is, and he is an alcoholic and a chain smoker. The job he works pays less than $20 per hour; so even if he were able to work overtime, he would never gross more than $3,200 per month. Their idea of retirement was owning a mortgage-free house in Las Vegas.

"They own a home in the Bay Area valued at $650,000, and their loan on that home is still $460,000. Their housing expense alone is about $2,100 each month; so every month the wife is not working, they have to pull money out of their 401K.

"On top of all that, her husband is not in good health. She actually said, 'I'm afraid for my husband. He just looks sick, and I'm afraid his body is giving out.'

"I talked to that lady very directly, and I said, 'Here's what I'm going to do for you. We're going to run a hundred miles an hour so you can replace his income before your husband's illness prevents him from working.' Then I said, 'Do you want to keep working? If you don't want to work, listen closely to what I tell you. It's your only way out.'

"She listened. She understood. She agreed to try my plan. Now, she is well on her way to a decent retirement. I really believe that it's probable her husband will live for a long time; but if he dies a few years from now, she will have to deal only with her sorrow. She will not have to deal both with her sorrow and also with utter poverty.

"This, to me, is an example of a person who didn't have the highest academic intelligence; but her willingness to receive advice revealed sufficient financial intelligence to transform her retirement."

Eric said, "In a way, we're talking about separate intelligences. What you're saying is that someone can be highly educated and highly trained in one area, but that doesn't necessarily mean that the person has been properly trained about money. And a person can have such a limited amount of education and training that he still earns low wages after decades of work, but he can still make financial decisions that can really put him ahead. Thinking about money is a separate item. It is a different kind of intelligence."

"The example I just gave you shows that a married couple spent literally decades working and paying bills. But when this lady took a few hours of her time to listen to a good financial strategy and then decided to follow the plan, the financial intelligence she gained in an hour got her further ahead than the job she had worked for decades.

"Now, there's also food intelligence," I teased, "and the decisions I make at this farmer's market are going to transform my taste buds for the next few days!"

"Megan and I have been talking," Eric said, "and we're going to follow the advice you've given us. If you don't mind, when you get back to work, we're going to drive to your office and put ourselves on the path to financial freedom."

"Oh, but then I'll be all confused!" I exclaimed. "I've been talking to you while I'm on a mini-vacation. So when you come to my office, I might think I'm on vacation again!"

"No," Megan disagreed, "we'll be sure to work you hard when we come in. Besides, even though there's nothing wrong with San Jose, there's just no place like Half Moon Bay."

"Well, when you come," I said, "you'll have to bring me some fresh fish from Pillar Point Harbor. Not only will it save me a trip, it will be a good reminder of our first accidental meeting."

CHAPTER 7

PREPARING TO INVEST

ACFTER THOROUGHLY ENJOYING MYSELF at the local market and talking with Eric and Megan, I returned to our hotel. Without being in any particular hurry, Carol, Jan, Herna, and I began to get our things together so we could pack the Hummer and drive home.

"I have this problem," Carol complained. "I always forget to allow enough extra space in my luggage for all the extra items I purchase when I go shopping. In this case, I have an extra difficulty. I am so relaxed from all the spa treatments that I really don't feel like spending the energy it takes to fit all these items in my suitcase!"

We all laughed. "Oh, I don't think you're the only one who is sometimes guilty of over-shopping," Herna said. "One of my friends suggested that carrying heavy shopping bags was the best way for me to work out!"

Jan chimed in. "Cristina, I think what we're all really getting at is that you have been so generous during this trip that we have way too much stuff.

But more than that, we've received the kindness of friendship, something that can't be purchased in any store or market. Mom and I are so glad you let us come along on this mini-vacation to Half Moon Bay."

Before too much more time went by, we had called the bellman, loaded our vehicle, and were on the way back home. As we were driving through the beautiful mountains back towards Highway 101, Jan started asking questions. She was curious about my conversations with Eric and Megan.

"Cristina," Jan began, "I understand that you have been talking to Eric and Megan about investing, and I know your career has a lot to do with helping people make great investments. But here is my question. Are there things people can do to get themselves ready? Can people do things that will make it easier for you to work with them?"

"Absolutely," I answered. "I believe everyone has possibilities, but some people just don't take them. But there are a few relatively simple things people can do in order to make investing easier."

"Can you tell me the most important things?" Jan asked.

RESERVES

"In my opinion, every person should start a savings account so he has reserves. In the first place, having some money in the bank makes you look stronger to the people who will loan you money. Of course, it would be nice if you had millions and millions of dollars in the bank; but you don't need millions to be in a better position. On a regular basis, you should try to put money in savings.

"Every person is going to experience times of financial emergency. Perhaps an unexpected home repair will come up. Perhaps a tragic family loss will require travel. It's hard to predict what all will come your way, but it's great to have some money in reserve when such times come."

Jan interjected, "I can understand that you need reserves just because of life, but how does that help you as an investor?"

"You see," I continued, "just as you will experience unexpected emergencies as an ordinary person, you will experience unexpected emergencies as an investor. Let's suppose you own a rental property that is leased on a month-to-month basis. If you have a tenant who moves out, it might take a month or two to replace that person. If you had money in reserve, you wouldn't panic about how to make the mortgage payment on your rental property.

"As I was talking with Megan and Eric, I was explaining investment options for people who have already built up a considerable amount of equity in their house. However, I also have methods of working with people who are just buying their first home. It's great to have a lot of equity to work with, but you don't have to wait. Since I can help you get started with investing much earlier than you might think, it's great to be prepared for this by having some money set aside for reserves.

"Financial institutions give higher credit scores for people who have money in the bank. They understand that these people are better prepared for life's little emergencies; therefore, it is less risky to loan them money."

"How much money should someone put in the bank?" Jan asked.

"Of course, different people give different answers to that question. But the best thing to do is to set aside a little money every week or every month. There is a huge difference between people who spend all the money they have and people who don't spend all the money they have. The people who save just have a different mindset. They have to be a little less impulsive. They have to be a little more careful.

"People who continually spend every dime they have tend to feel desperate for money all the time. They deceive themselves by constantly justifying why they have to spend all their money and increase their consumer debt. Some people who spend all the money they have make $50,000 per year. Some make $100,000 per year. Some make $200,000 per year. But it doesn't matter. No matter how much they make, they always feel financially strapped. They tend to blame their circumstances or 'hope for a better day tomorrow,' and they never see the nature of their own problem."

Jan summarized, "So saving some money is an extremely important first step?"

"That's exactly right," I answered. "By saving money, you are increasing your credit score and you are preparing for life's emergencies. That's a great path to take if you're hoping to become financially free."

PAY ON TIME

We continued to wind through the beautiful mountains, enjoying the sights and enjoying each other's company. But Jan had become quite intrigued with the whole idea of investing. The more we talked, the more she wanted to know. I sensed that a very important light was turning on inside her mind.

"Cristina," Jan said, "I understand the idea of saving money so you have reserves. What is another important thing people can do to prepare themselves for investing?"

"There is no question about the fact that paying your bills on time is really important," I answered. "Years ago, I talked with a receptionist in an insurance office who told me they have some clients who bring their payments in fifteen days late every single month. They never pay on time. They never pay thirty days late. They always bring their payment in fifteen days late.

"If people can pay their bills every month and can pay their bills consistently every month, then they have the ability to pay their bills on time every month. They just need to add organization and determination to their lives. When you pay your bills on time, you demonstrate character and credibility. And if you hope to become an investor, having character and credibility is worth a lot."

"Why does it work this way?" Jan asked.

"Lending institutions make money by loaning money. But when they loan money, they have to get it back. It's easy to understand why a bank would lose money if it loaned $10,000 to a person who never paid it back. But when the bank loans money to people who are late, they have to spend extra money sending reminders and generally asking people to pay their bills on time. Since there are plenty of people who do pay their bills on time, banks feel they should charge higher fees for customers who cause them grief—and they won't loan money at all to people if they have serious fears about getting it back.

"Though it may seem simple, one of the very best things people can do to prepare themselves as investors is to pay their bills on time, every time."

PATIENCE

"Another secret of investing, Jan," I said, "is to be patient. In California, we have some magnificent redwood trees. Some of these trees are hundreds of years old. They're wonderful. They're beautiful. But they didn't appear in a moment. It took time.

"As you approach the world of investing, it is wise to invest in an aggressive growth market like real estate. But it is not a good idea to spend time in get-rich-quick schemes. For everyone who wins a pile of money gambling, untold dozens of people lose money—and many even become bankrupt. For everyone who makes a few dollars on get-rich-quick businesses, there are many people who lose money. Many times, these people even lose the desire to keep trying.

"There is an old adage that says, 'all good things come to those who wait.' And it's true. When you purchase your first investment property, you're not going to become a multi-millionaire the first day. But as you nurture your investments, you will see them grow. With a little bit of patience, you can bring your financial destiny under control."

"Is it true," Jan asked, "that some people hurt themselves by becoming glitzy too soon? I've heard that, but I'm not really sure what it means."

"I'm glad you asked," I answered. "Sure. Some people try to act like rich folks, but they don't lay the right foundation. Let me explain.

"As you know, I currently own a vehicle manufactured by Rolls-Royce. It is really a fabulous automobile. Let's suppose someone sees this car and says, 'Wow! It must be nice to be rich. I want to live like that. In fact, I want to have a nice car so badly that I'm going shopping right now for the nicest thing I can afford.'

"So that person takes his money to the car dealership. He finds a car. He purchases the nicest vehicle he can afford. As he drives the car off the lot, he might be thinking, 'This is great! Now I know how it feels to be rich. Just give me five years, and I'll have this car paid for—this is wonderful!'

"Actually, there is a huge difference between that person and me. Because I was a patient person, I invested my money first. I had money in savings. I purchased rental properties. I did everything I could to become a good steward of my money. Because of that, I now have a lot of income every month. Not only do I earn a salary from my real estate company, I also receive money from my investments. I invested my money first, so it's easier for me to spend huge amounts of money on new vehicles. The person I just described spent his money first. Instead of putting money into investments that would yield great rewards over time, he spent all his money on items that will depreciate. At the end of another five years, my investments will have multiplied even more; so I'll have even more money to spend. But at the end of that same five years, he will definitely need another car; and he won't have any more money than he had when he made his last purchase."

"Oh, I see," Jan noted. "Both the patient investor and the impulsive spender buy cars, but the one invests money first and buys nice things later; the other buys nice things first and never invests money."

"Yes," I said, "and that makes an incredible difference in the financial futures of these two people. Really, it all boils down to patience. You need to make wise decisions, and you need to be patient. When you put those two things together, you can make a huge difference in your financial future."

MINDSET

Jan was making a list as we talked. "Okay," she said, "It's a good idea to save money. You need to pay your bills on time every time. And you need to be patient. Are there any other really important things to know?"

"I talk about this so often," I said. "I talked about this with Megan and Eric while we were in Half Moon Bay. I talk about this with my staff and with my clients. It is so very important to understand the importance of mindset.

"There are some people who are positively charged. They are winners. They are optimistic. They are positive. There are some people who don't seem to be overly positive, and they don't seem to really be negative. They just drift through life with an average mentality. Of course, there are people who are quite negative. They believe they are in a bad situation, and they act as though their lives are completely hopeless.

"If you want to be a successful investor, I believe it's important to develop a positive spirit. It helps to read good books about having a positive spirit. It helps to be with people who have a positive spirit. It helps to develop your own dreams and work towards them with a positive spirit.

"I've said it so many times, and I'll say it as long as I can. There is a better way to live than just to work a job and pay the bills. Though no investment is risk-free, there are sound ways to make investments—especially real estate investments—that can transform your financial life. It's actually possible to work a job just because you want to work the job. It's actually possible to be in a position where working is optional.

"I think it's important to develop the mental ability to see yourself in a new condition. I truly believe that people need to be able to picture themselves in a different, better world. If they can do this, they can learn to be financially free."

FINAL THOUGHTS

"This has been a very interesting conversation to me, Cristina," Jan said. "I guess I never really spent that much time thinking about it, but I have believed that being wealthy—what you call being financially free—was something that was extremely difficult, something that only a few people would ever be able to figure out. But so much of what you're explaining isn't really that hard at all. It's simple, but it seems to be so important."

"You're very right, Jan. I completely agree. Certainly it helps to be a genius. And it's true that some people simply have the ability to make more money than others. But we've all heard stories of geniuses that died in poverty. And some of the wealthiest people in the world were certainly not geniuses. When it comes to financial freedom, it is possible for average, ordinary people to invest. And by investing, especially by leveraging money in the real estate market, it is possible for most people to live a life they never dreamed was possible."

As we were driving south on Highway 101, I began thinking of my mini-vacation in Half Moon Bay. I thought of Eric and Megan. I thought of my conversation with Jan. I began thinking about so many clients I have been honored to serve all these years.

I had just enjoyed a relaxing getaway that many people will never be able to experience. I wasn't able to enjoy these things because I was born rich or because I got lucky one day in a get-rich-quick scheme. I was blessed. I was able to learn a few simple principles of investing and a few simple attitudes in life, and I learned that these seemingly simple things made a world of difference.

Almost anyone who has owned a home for several years can become an investor. But when people actually prepare to become investors, it can be that much easier. As we headed towards home, I had this thought over and over again: "Lord, please let me help as many people as I can." I have had many tremendous opportunities. Now, I want to have the joy of helping others find those same opportunities.

CHAPTER 8

CHOOSING AN AGENT

AS WE ARRIVED BACK at Carol's house in Santa Clara, I could feel that our mini-vacation was coming to an end; but I was in no particular hurry to get back to my normal business routine. After we had unloaded the luggage for Carol and Jan, Carol invited us into the kitchen where our conversation continued its cheerful course.

Carol was taking a leisurely look through her cabinets to see if she could find some little snack to place on the table when she said, "Cristina, that trip was a wonderful experience for Jan and me. As you know, Jan and I are blessed; and we have everything we need. But it would have been quite awhile before we could have taken a little excursion like that. I'm so thankful you called and invited us to go with you.

"At the same time," Carol continued, "I'm a little concerned about you."

"Me?" I was startled. "Why are you concerned about me?"

"I'm concerned," Carol said, "because we were all totally relaxing this weekend, but you spent a good deal of your time talking business to Eric and Megan. I know you were able to spend a long time in the spa, but I was wondering if your mind truly had time to relax because you seem to stumble into more business by accident than some people do on purpose!"

"I can assure you," I said confidently, "that I know how to escape when I need to. Actually, I love the work I do; and because of the unusual circumstances of literally meeting Megan by accident, I was able to add an interesting twist to my mini-vacation. If you understood how much I love my work and how much I enjoy helping people, you wouldn't be concerned about me at all. You would know that I had a great time, and talking with Megan and Eric added a delightful surprise to my trip."

"One thing is for sure," Carol concluded, "you are certainly cut out for your job. But I do have a question about Eric and Megan. If they decide to invest in real estate and they want to find a real estate agent closer to home, how would they go about it? Of course, I think they would be foolish not to take the time to drive to your office. But what is important about finding a good real estate agent?"

"Well most of the agents that you'll find out there, all they want to do is sell you a property. They're after what they can get from you. There's a big difference in an agent who wants to sell you a property so he can make a six-percent commission and an agent who has the vision and experience to see your road map to riches. You see, most real estate agents don't know how to find the right property that will be what you need for your long-term investments."

Carol asked, "Cristina, how many real estate agents do you think understand your powerhouse investment strategy? One out of ten? One out of a hundred? One out of a thousand?"

"I think one of a thousand," I answered. "You see, they may know how to sell a four-plex or a commercial property or a single-family residence. However, they don't seem to comprehend the right delivery. They don't seem to understand how to make the connections from point A to point B, then on to point C and to point D.

"I don't think most real estate agents can paint a picture of investment in the minds of their clients. When I sit down with people, I don't just provide them information about the first transaction we need to make. I show them the plan from the beginning all the way through to the end. One of the things I always explain to them is that my investment strategy will be able to lead them to early retirement.

"When I explain that early retirement will be an option and I have explained some of the strategies that will make this happen, the clients themselves experience a shift in their mindset. When they hear about early retirement, they begin to think, 'Oh, boy. I'm tired of working. This is going to be great. How can we get started in that process?' Because I have created a long-term mental image for them and they have begun to develop a positive mindset, our relationship is characterized by energetic goal setting that works well for everyone.

"After I gather the information I need from them, I explain that we have to begin with some baby steps, that we can't jump into the final phase all at once."

"So really," Carol observed, "a good agent has to be experienced with real estate, but he also has to be experienced in helping people mentally picture a good plan of attack."

"Yes, Carol, you are thinking right," I answered. "I have to explain that successful real estate investing has to be done phase by phase. I have to create a mental picture of the plan for them, and I do that by showing them the options they have—and the options they will have. I say, 'Here is the starting point. This is our first phase.'

"By the time we are ready to take the next step, my financial team has been able to work out loan details that give us specific financial options. When my clients have an investment goal and a positive attitude, I provide them with technical expertise in the real estate market; and everything begins humming right along."

PERSONAL EXPERIENCE

As we continued our little conversation, Carol began pouring tea for us. She always seemed to know just what would hit the spot. I have told her on many occasion that she could have made a small fortune as a chef.

"There is something, else, Carol," I said. "Most real estate agents don't know how to convert clients into investors. Through the years, I have had so many different people working for me; and some of them later went into real estate businesses of their own. In many cases, they listened to me and they even attended some of my seminars. But I don't believe they can explain it the same way I can."

"Do you really think so?" Carol asked. "I would think that, by working with you, a reasonably intelligent person would learn how to make a presentation."

"Oh, of course they can do a presentation," I explained, "but I don't think they can transfer the intensity and the reality of it. I don't think they can do that because they themselves have not experienced it. They have not taken themselves down the path of investment; and when you do something yourself, you learn things by experience that take on a totally new meaning.

"There is nothing wrong with book learning. I'm for it. There is nothing wrong with learning from others. That is very valuable. But I am wary of people who have learned by reading and learned by observing—but they have never learned by doing. If they haven't learned the principles of investing personally, I don't believe they have the kind of knowledge that will help them guide others through the investment process.

"There are even real estate agents who have personally purchased an investment property or two. They undoubtedly have more knowledge than those who have only heard about such strategies. But here is the big question: Have they achieved financial freedom for themselves? If they haven't achieved these goals in their own lives, how can you trust them to help you achieve your financial goals? To place confidence in such people is like having a blind guide. You may get somewhere, but it won't be down the road of riches.

"So how can an agent in his right mind really explain what he hasn't experienced? It's too theoretical. In a way, you're just dealing with a person who wants to make a sale, not a person who understands firsthand the art of real estate investment.

"As I deal with clients, I get questions all the time. They say, 'So, Cristina, since you're explaining this strategy to me, I suppose you have lots of properties?' And when they ask me that kind of question, I can honestly answer, 'Yes, I have been blessed to own dozens of properties.'

"I have clients who are somewhat skeptical, and they are concerned about my credibility. These clients may say, 'Do you own the building that your office is in?' When they ask questions like that, I can answer with confidence, 'Yes, I own this building. And I own this building along with many, many other properties all around the world because I understand real estate investment by personal experience. I practice what I preach.'

"I think it's very important to work with somebody who is already successful in real estate investment. I think it's very important to have an agent who has already been down that path personally. There is simply no knowledge that can replace personal experience."

KNOWLEDGE OF PROPERTIES

As she was sipping her chamomile tea, Carol said, "Cristina, I understand that a good real estate agent needs to have personal experience. But I have also noticed that you seem like a walking encyclopedia when it comes to real estate properties. Why does your knowledge of the properties matter?"

"Knowledge is important," I explained to Carol, "because the people with whom you come in contact are smart too. They know whether I am bluffing or just guessing. And the sellers are especially smart. Sellers say, 'Hey, don't you need to see my house first? Where did you come up with this value if you haven't even been inside my house?' But I know the housing prices throughout the Bay Area. I know those prices like the palm of my hand.

"I maintain a knowledge of the market. I study it. I deal with it day by day. I see daily reports on at least 25 to 30 different properties that have been analyzed by specialists. On my desk every day is a listing of all available properties, both single-family residences and multiple units. I read those reports constantly so I know what the trends are.

"For example, you could mention a four-plex in Campbell—or in North San Jose, South San Jose, Sunnyvale, or Santa Clara—and if you told me the number of bedrooms, the square footage and the rental incomes, I would be able to tell you the approximate price immediately, even without referring to any of my reports.

"If a real estate agent doesn't have the ability to carry all these numbers in his head, it is very possible that the client can miss some great deals. In order to be on the cutting edge of the real estate market, it's vitally important to know the details."

FINANCING

"The last thing, Carol," I said, "is that I believe it's very important for a real estate agent to have great financing tools available. The agent needs to be very knowledgeable about the world of finance."

"Cristina, do you have more options for financing because you own your own finance company?" Carol asked.

"Absolutely. But it's not just a matter of having more options. Because I am the owner of my own finance company, I have a greater knowledge of the business. Again, there is more credibility when you own your own company than there is when you simply work well with another company. Of course, very few real estate agents own their own finance company.

"And though it may seem like a little thing, it's helpful if a real estate agent is good with numbers. I've seen many real estate agents—even some who worked for me—who would always call to get numbers from financial institutions. Personally, I have been blessed with a good sense of numbers; and I have crunched numbers for a long, long time. Thus, I can know a property price; and I can instantly calculate in my head what the monthly payments will be on the mortgage, and I can instantly determine what the monthly property taxes will be.

"When there are unusual circumstances, it is very beneficial to my clients that I own my own finance company. With that kind of ability, we can often work through the complexities of investment real estate transactions and find some kind of workable solution."

"From what you're telling me," Carol said, "it seems like you're a good real estate doctor. If you know the price of a house anywhere in the Bay Area right off the top of your head and you can calculate the mortgage and taxes right off the top of your head, you're like a doctor who intimately knows the details of your medical condition and can quickly get down to the business of helping you.

"But who would want to go to a doctor that didn't understand the human condition? If the patient said,

'I think I'm having trouble with my liver,' can you imagine how he would feel if the doctor replied, 'Hold on for just a minute. I want to look in my books to be sure I know what the liver is. After I study this for awhile, I will be able to prescribe some appropriate treatments.' That would be clearly horrible."

"I think you're exactly right," I said. "Many people would not put up with that kind of doctor, but they employ real estate agents who don't have quick, up-to-the-minute knowledge of real estate prices and financing. By having this knowledge available to me instantly, I can concentrate on the needs of my clients and come up with creative solutions that can help them become financially free.

"When your agent has a lot of experience, knows the market well, and knows the world of finances well, he can simply do what others cannot do. When an agent doesn't own his own building, doesn't own his own finance company, doesn't personally own dozens of real estate properties, doesn't have intimate knowledge of real estate prices, and doesn't have instant knowledge of loan rates—well, this agent could be called Mr.

Doesn't. People who invest in real estate don't need an agent who *doesn't* have all these things. They need an agent who *does!*

"If you have a real estate agent who doesn't have all these qualities, there's an old proverb that definitely applies: BUYER, BEWARE!"

With that, we finished our conversation. And just a few moments later, Herna and I were on our way again. Our mini-vacation was all but over. I had relaxed, but I also had the satisfaction of knowing that I had helped more people learn something about the joys of real estate investing.

I still have great faith in people, and I believe that there are thousands, even millions, of people who can improve their lives if they have the proper education and if they work with the right people. Understanding a good real estate investment strategy is important, but working with a great real estate agent is also extremely vital.

CHAPTER 9

GIVING

OUR MINI-VACATION WAS OVER. It was Monday morning, and Herna and I were back to work in the office. We had enjoyed our time at Half Moon Bay, and it was always delightful to be with Carol and Jan. One of the privileges of being financially free is that you have the pleasure of giving to others. By sharing part of what you received, you can experience a special joy that is only available for people who give.

Herna, standing quietly by my desk, made an interesting observation. "It seems to me, Cristina, that knowing about real estate investing and having the right mindset is important. But it seems that people who learn to give somehow have better results."

"I agree, Herna. When people love only themselves, they certainly can work hard to achieve success in business. But when people care about others, they find something greater than themselves; and it can cause them to achieve results that are far greater."

"Cristina," Herna said, "explain to me what you were thinking when you decided to donate a major building to a local college."

"Herna, you have worked with me all these years; and you know that I have always worked really hard. Somehow, I have always had an inner drive that makes me want to succeed. I have never found joy in being Number Two. I've always wanted to be Number One.

"When I first came to the United States, part of my goal was to help my family. I felt that I had many opportunities, just by being in America. I had a strong drive to succeed. Of course, I have enjoyed many financial blessings personally. I have purchased so many wonderful things. But my success has never been separated from my family.

"However, when I decided to build a multi-million-dollar building for a local college, that decision really pushed me. I knew the building would bear my name, so I wanted it to be right. I knew I would have the money to pay for the building, but I wanted to keep the rest of my life in order at the same time.

"There were times I thought of the college students who would use the building. I would think of how they would be busy with their studies, and they would have bright hopes and dreams for the future. As I began to think of them and the potential of their lives, it drove me to stretch myself. It made me find new ways of thinking and doing business.

"To be honest, there were times when I began to second-guess myself. I would think, 'Cristina, why are you giving away millions of dollars? What will this do to your own financial security? What will this mean for your retirement?' And so, inside myself, there was sometimes a battle. But when I let myself focus on giving, I was amazed at the opportunities that came my way and the creativity that I developed.

"Before the building was even finished, it seemed that I kept being flooded with blessings. It was almost as though there is a law of the universe that makes it impossible to give without receiving. In the Bible, it says, 'It is more blessed to give than to receive.' But in my own experience, I not only found more happiness when I gave, but I also found that I kept making more money when I gave.

"So, to answer your question, Herna, my business flourished when I began to focus on the needs of others. When I began to help them more, it seemed that I was helping myself more, even though that wasn't my original goal."

Herna responded, "Of course, people who are selfish—and perhaps even criminal—can make a lot of money sometimes. What do you think the difference is when you live to give for worthy causes?"

"First of all, Herna, there are many worthy causes; and different people have a desire to support different causes. Sometimes, people simply have a desire to help their families. Perhaps a father wants to pay his daughter's way through school. Perhaps a grandmother wants to obtain world-class medical care for her ailing grandchild. Some people sponsor the arts. Many people support their church.

"I suppose there could be a little argument among people about which cause is the most worthy. But it seems to me that when people get involved in a truly worthy cause, it enables them to freely open all their creativity and all their industry. They don't have to worry about getting caught doing something wrong because they have dedicated themselves to something that is inherently right.

"But I think people who are selfish somehow realize that there is something wrong with their approach to life. Of course, if they ever cross the line into criminal activity, it is very clear that they are part of something that is completely wrong. Because of this, they can try very hard to make a lot of money; but there is always something they must hide. Their spirit cannot be free and open because if they truly opened up they would have to deal with how ugly their selfishness is.

"To me, it seems that nature itself works against the selfish soul. Everyone who works hard receives some benefit from his labor, but it seems that people who give simply encounter more opportunities, more blessings, and more financial freedom."

"Do you think," Herna asked, "that people who are selfish tend to make wrong decisions?"

"Well," I said, "I don't think they do all the time. But ultimately, what is in our heart catches up with us. When people live their entire lives thinking, 'It's all about me,' it's bound to catch up with them. At some point, the ugliness of their selfishness comes out as the ugliness of a bad business decision. Because they don't experience the freedom that comes as we dedicate our lives to others, they sometimes grasp at things that appeal to their selfish nature. When they grab the rod of selfishness, they find that it is truly a serpent; and it seems to bite them every time."

"But, Cristina, very few people have the ability to donate a multi-million-dollar building to an institution of higher learning," Herna noted. "In what ways can giving affect ordinary people?"

"Everyone can give," I said. "When a child in elementary school gives a flower to her mother, that is giving just as much as donating a million dollars to a charity. Giving can happen in an infinite number of ways, and all those ways are good.

"Herna, you know I enjoy giving to my church. I give on a regular basis to support the regular program of the church. Sometimes I give very large amounts of money to support special projects. But I also give my time.

"On Saturdays, I often spend time visiting underprivileged children, and I encourage them to come to church. When they come to church, they not only have a chance to be spiritually enriched, they also have a chance to think about life in a different way and to know the hope that is provided by the good news of the Gospel. Many of these children are trapped in poverty, and they rarely see much outside their immediate area. But when their lives are touched with kindness, they begin to understand that there is a vast world out there—much larger than they ever imagined—and their lives begin to grow.

"When you give, you sometimes give cash. Sometimes, you give time. Sometimes, you give thoughtfulness. But no matter what kind of giving it is, it is still giving. It is still thinking of others. It is still selfless.

"It seems to me that a child who will not give his mother a flower can easily become a teen who will not volunteer to work at a school fund-raiser. The teen who won't help at school can easily become an adult who won't give a dollar to his church. The adult who won't give a dollar can easily become a husband who refuses to meet the emotional needs of his wife. The unkind husband can easily become a cruel businessman who only thinks of his own needs—and the idea of giving in any way seems to be completely lost.

"But the child who will give his mother a flower can easily become a teen who will cheerfully volunteer to work at his school fund-raisers. Then it's easy for this teen to develop into an adult who enjoys supporting his church financially. This adult then finds it easy to think of his wife in a tender, thoughtful way; and he learns to meet all her needs. Finally, this man becomes a person who finds joy in helping all of society. With such people, giving has become a way of life; therefore, giving large amounts of money is relatively easy for them because they've developed a pattern of giving throughout their lives.

"I've never seen a person give a million dollars who didn't first give a dollar, and I've never seen a person give a helping hand to someone in need who didn't first offer a friendly smile. But when I find someone who cares for others—both his own family and society in general—I discover a person who accomplishes more in every area, even in the area of real estate investment."

"I never really thought about this until now," Herna said. "But even on this trip, you were giving and receiving. You decided that you wanted to give a special treat to Carol and her daughter; but as you did that, you met a fine couple who will probably become long-term clients of yours. If we look at it strictly in terms of dollars and cents, you spent a lot of money on Carol and Jan; but as you work with Eric and Megan, you will earn more in commission than you spent on the trip."

"That is precisely my point, Herna! It seems that there is this wonderful law of nature that makes it impossible to give away something without getting more in return. So often, people operate in fear. They want to hold on to every dollar. They do not give. They think that being stingy will enable them to keep their riches.

"But the truth of the matter is that you always gain more when you give than you hold on to when you refuse to give. Of course, you need to be wise in your giving. But most people don't need to learn how to give carefully—they need to learn how to give at all!

"Right now, I can think of so many people that I have tried to help. When I began trying to help these people, I hardly had a decent existence here in America. But through the years, I have given and given and given; and it seems that the more I give away, the more there is for me to keep.

"Besides all that, my giving keeps my heart and mind open. As I work day by day, I work in freedom—not in the bondage of selfishness!"

"You need to hide, Cristina," Herna said. "I think I hear John once again, and he may well want to do another carat count!"

We both laughed. It is a joy to work in an office with good people who believe in being industrious and efficient. It is a joy to work a job that enables me to positively impact the lives of all my clients. Most of all, it is a joy to work knowing that I will have more and more opportunities to invest in the lives of others by giving.

CHAPTER 10

GETTING STARTED

I T WAS THURSDAY AFTERNOON, and I was working at my desk when the receptionist called. With her typically cheerful tone, she said, "Cristina, Eric and Megan are here to see you."

I was more than excited to see this couple. We had met by accident in Half Moon Bay, but I could tell they had a great deal of curiosity about the whole concept of investing. When some people hear about investing, they are interested at first; but then the whole idea somehow frightens them, and they don't follow through. On the other hand, there are those who hear about investing, the seeds of real estate investment are sown, and then the whole idea begins to develop a life of its own. There is growth. Then there is great growth.

I left my office with great eagerness and walked towards our reception area. I could hear their voices. As soon as our eyes met, Megan enthusiastically announced, "Cristina, we brought you a present!"

"I love presents! What is it?" I asked.

"Of all things, we decided to bring you some fresh produce from the farmers' market! We really couldn't afford an expensive gift that was appropriate for a multi-millionaire, but we knew you loved the market—and everyone loves great food! If these carrots taste like the ones we bought, you're going to have a great time deciding the best place to use them."

"This is terrific," I said. "I think I'll go to Half Moon Bay more often to see if I can find more nice people! It's not every day that people bring me produce from the farmers' market!"

We were talking like old friends as they made themselves comfortable in my office. I pulled out a folder and said, "Megan and Eric, I have good news for you! You already talked with the people in my finance company, so I know just exactly the kind of equity we can put to work for you. In this packet right here, I have the information on three absolutely perfect properties for you!"

"Do you mean that we don't have to start by viewing potential properties all over the Bay Area?"

Eric asked. "We were thinking that you were going to spend several days driving us all over town!"

"Of course, if you want to do that, you can. But most of my clients are interested in making money, not in endlessly driving from one property to another. So I try to do the homework for you. My analysts have studied every listed property in the Bay Area to find the investment properties that work best in your situation. When I evaluated all the possibilities, I selected what I thought were the best three for you to consider.

"Once you purchase your first investment property, we will hold on to this property for awhile, and then you will see your investment grow. Once that begins to happen, there will be so many options for you! When you begin the journey down this road, I know you're going to be thrilled with the results."

Megan seemed to be bubbling with excitement, "Let's go see the properties. I can't wait to sign the papers and get the ball rolling!"

"Absolutely!" Eric said. "I'm ready to get this done so we can move on to the next options as soon as possible!"

"Hold on, hold on," I said to them. I couldn't help but smile at their enthusiasm. "Let's get first things first. One of my assistants will show you these properties. Your dreams are coming, Eric. But we have to go one step at a time."

After they had seen the properties and decided which one to buy, I was able to explain the features of the property to Eric and Megan. And I was able to tell them possible next steps.

"How long will we need to own this before we move on to the next step?" Eric asked.

"As I mentioned before, Eric, we have to play this by ear, but it won't be too long, depending on the market."

We looked at numbers. We looked at comparable properties. It was exciting to see the facts of the transaction come together in front of their eyes. It was very clear that they were excited about real estate investment, and they seemed to completely agree that this property was going to work for them. Megan liked the idea that it was fairly close by, so she could "keep her eye on it."

"The only question I have," Eric said, "is why did it take me so long to meet you in the first place? By using the equity we have already accumulated in our home, it's going to be easy for us to achieve some financial goals that we both never considered. If we had only known the information you gave us, we could have already gotten started!"

"No, no, Eric, I am wondering why it took me so long to meet you. It's very evident that you are good, hard-working people; and I think it's important that people like you learn methods of real estate investing that can make them financially free. I'm thankful I was able to tell you about real estate investment. Some people live their whole lives without ever coming across this knowledge. To me, that is terrible and tragic."

Within a few moments, they had signed the necessary documents; and they were well on their way to becoming successful investors. "Now that we've taken care of all this," I told them, "let me shake hands with Mr. and Mrs. Investor!"

FINAL THOUGHTS

The basic principles of real estate investing are easy enough to understand. It is important, though, to work with a real estate agent that has a thorough understanding of the market, someone who can help you achieve success.

It has been my privilege to sell thousands of properties. I long ago passed one billion dollars in sales. I have been able to work with some fabulous clients, and so many of them have become financially free. It has been a truly rewarding experience to see them reach goals they never thought were possible.

If you are ready to begin your personal journey in real estate investment, I would be honored to answer your questions and to assist you any way I can. If you have read this book, you understand the basic principles of real estate investment. Now, it's time to get started!

Cristina Martinez

THE CRISTINA MARTINEZ COMPANY
1699 N. Capitol Avenue
San Jose, CA 95132
(408) 934-2000
richesmyway@cristinapowerhouse.com
www.cristinapowerhouse.com